Words That Make Sense

by Dr. Jaky B. & Kendra D. Banks
RIB Publishing
Baltimore, Maryland

Copyright 2026

Published by

RIB Publishing
1001 Frederick Road, Ste. 3125
Catonsville, Maryland 21211

Printed in the United States of America
All reproduction and duplication rights
reserved. Prior written approval from
the publisher is required.

Acknowledgments

From Dr. Jaky B. - I would like to thank everyone who has given me words of encouragement over the-years: the late Mary Gladys Jones, Cynthia Jacobs, Alexis Dashield, the late Frank Perdue, Lee Whaley, Cynthia Polk, the late Randolph Outten, Barbara Mayes Colbert Jefferson, Dalena Braswell, Robert Mayes Sr., the Honorable Edward Taylor, Meg Schomann, Richard Bebee, Ph.D, the late Marion Birkhead, Mary Ashanti, the late Reverend Vaughn P. Johnson, the late Cora Goslee, the late Phyllis Dawes and the late Maurice Crawford. Plus my Uncle Julius and Aunt Doris Polk Chandler, my Uncle Morris Polk and Aunt Iva Polk Brooken for always supporting my projects! No questions! Actually—I learn from everyone I have a conversation with so thank you for sharing. ❤

From Kendra- Grandma your baby girl is a Gigi now. You instilled into the both of us life lessons that assisted me into womanhood. I miss you every day the sky is blue and will continue to make you proud. Thank you to every ancestor that has crossed the plane before me and to my angels on this earth: Jody, Kristy, Brandi, Tashae, Maxen and Seven.

Dedication

In memory of our grandmother and mother Mrs. Naomi Polk Banks and all mothers who have shared their own proverbs with loved ones. Thank you for caring and sharing. We appreciate that you led by example and showered us with love, truth and grace. We were strong willed girls yet we listened because your wisdom was evident. Your words ring true everyday.

We believe this book will help some young person to understand more reality and stay focused. We believe this will help somebody to see the bigger picture of life. We believe this will inspire someone to become a better entrepreneur, a better parent, companion. We hope this will help someone to understand the role and impact of race in our everyday lives. We hope this will help everyone to understand the importance of spirituality in our lives.

Peace & Love,
Dr. Jaky B. &
Kendra D. Banks

Introduction

Naomi's Proverbs: A Black Mother Speaks is an-acute, unique look into wisdom given from a Black mother to her brown-skinned, short-hair daughter, Dr. Jaky B., who grew up during the Civil Rights Movement.
The book touches topics of racism, marriage, family, parenting,
business, church, spirituality, education and more.
It is uncut, real and offers no apology
for how a family had to survive then and now.
Enjoy the book.
Carry it with you.
It's sassy.
It's practical.
It makes sense.
It's real.
It's prophetic.
It applies just as much today!

It wasn't easy being Black in 1960 and it isn't in 2026. Yet. Still proud. Still achieving..

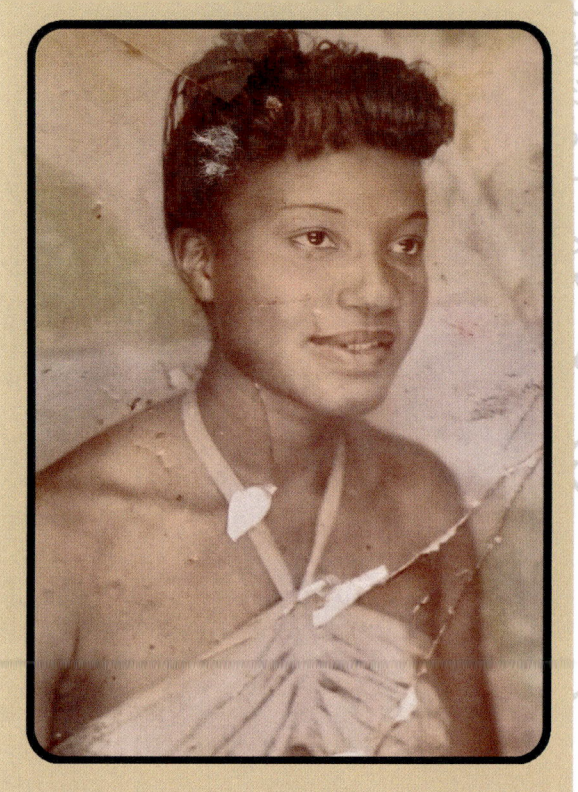

**The Late Naomi I. Polk Banks
Circa 1950s**
This is one of my favorite photographs of my mother because it shows her independent nature for her era. *Dr. J.*

On Business, Work and Finances

Naomi's Proverbs

Your best friends are God and your wallet.

A Black Mother Speaks — Page 2

Naomi's Proverbs

> The white man needed my labor and I needed a paycheck.

A Black Mother Speaks

Naomi's Proverbs

When you go to ask the white man for some money, always ask for more than what you need because he's only going to give you enough to get into trouble.

A Black Mother Speaks

Naomi's Proverbs

I made up my mind that I would never clean white people's houses. I seen how they treated my momma and I knew I could never do what she did and keep a job.

A Black Mother Speaks

Naomi's Proverbs

The average poor person who walks around with money in his pocket ain't paying no bills; all he is doing is wasting his money.

A Black Mother Speaks

Naomi's Proverbs

People respected us because we had a business. When the police came to arrest my husband for using a gun to break up a fight, I shot a pistol at the ceiling. I was very pregnant at the time and I was determined they were not going to take my husband away. I don't know why they didn't arrest me that night.

A Black Mother Speaks

Naomi's Proverbs

Pay your bills first. If you don't your money will be gone and you still won't have paid any bills.

Naomi's Proverbs

If a person has a title, give them respect for the title even if you don't like the person.

A Black Mother Speaks   Page 9

Naomi's Proverbs

Some women don't like me to this day because my husband had a business and I'd be dressed up everyday, ready to wait on them as they came in from the fields. I was just lucky.

Naomi's Proverbs

When people have money in their pocket, you can't tell them when and where to spend it. In business, you are always taking a chance.

Naomi's Proverbs

In order to have a crowd for a dance, we'd have to put posters up in small towns from Delaware all the way down to the Virginia line. That way, a handful of people from here and there would eventually make up a crowd. That's how we made our money. We just couldn't depend on the people in our own community.

Naomi's Proverbs

The average Black person ain't going to lose his job for you. But after you speak up and get a pay raise or something, they're the first ones in the white man's office talking about they do the same thing you do.

Race and Color

Naomi's Proverbs

Black folk just won't stick together.

A Black Mother Speaks

Naomi's Proverbs

Light-skinned Black people will call you black in a minute.

A Black Mother Speaks   Page 16

Naomi's Proverbs

The average white man doesn't think the Black person should have anything.

A Black Mother Speaks

Naomi's Proverbs

Most white people think Black people are stupid.

A Black Mother Speaks   Page 18

On Marriage and Relationships

Naomi's Proverbs

When people cheat in a marriage it takes the sweetness away from a marriage.

Naomi's Proverbs

Don't start nothing you can't finish. However you start off a relationship, that's how it's going to be.

Naomi's Proverbs

Men act like you ain't never supposed to get tired.

A Black Mother Speaks   Page 23

Naomi's Proverbs

Treat a man with a long handle spoon; you'll get along with him better.

Naomi's Proverbs

Always dress nice so your husband will get used to you leaving home fixed up.

A Black Mother Speaks — Page 25

Naomi's Proverbs

Be careful about accepting money and gifts from a man; he might think he owns you.

Naomi's Proverbs

Don't tell a man all your business.

A Black Mother Speaks   Page 27

Naomi's Proverbs

Most men don't want you to spend any money for clothes, yet they always want you to look nice.

Naomi's Proverbs

Even a piece of a man is better than no man at all especially if he helps you a little. Ain't no need to keep jumping from man to man. Ain't none of them perfect.

Naomi's Proverbs

Marriage is just an understanding between two people; it can be a very beautiful thing.

Naomi's Proverbs

My husband always believed in a woman taking some time for herself.

Naomi's Proverbs

Don't marry no ugly people because I don't want no ugly grandchildren.

Naomi's Proverbs

Every time we made friends with a couple, the woman would always end up trying to sleep with my husband.

Naomi's Proverbs

Just because I was a widow woman I wasn't supposed to have the same things as married couples. They'd get so jealous.

Naomi's Proverbs

Dr. Jaky B. - *My legacies!!!* My daughter, my son and his wife and their two children, my grandsons Maxen and Seven.

"My mother's words provided balance. I didn't land too badly in life."

"I took her advice and considered looks in selecting a spouse."

Naomi's Proverbs

Most people come to church with nothing and go home with nothing. If you don't bring nothing in with you, ain't nothing going home with you.

Naomi's Proverbs

Don't let nothing or nobody run you away from your church; you're there to serve God and not the people.

Naomi's Proverbs

My momma always made us go to church on Sunday morning no matter how late we stayed up or what we did on Saturday night.

A Black Mother Speaks

Naomi's Proverbs

Old folks are set in their ways. If their hearts weren't right before they get sick, they are going to be even meaner after they get sick.

Naomi's Proverbs

God loves the truth.

Naomi's Proverbs

Why take somebody to church after they're dead and gone and stretch 'em across the front of the church, when while they were alive they didn't even take themselves? Then the family sits there acting like the preacher is supposed to preach the dead person into Heaven.

Naomi's Proverbs

Sometimes people on the street will do more for you than people in the church.

A Black Mother Speaks   Page 43

Naomi's Proverbs

I've had a good life. God has been good.

A Black Mother Speaks   Page 44

Naomi's Proverbs

Some people are so evil; you'll lose your religion fooling around with them. Just pray for them and speak to everybody.

Naomi's Proverbs

Some folks just can't accept their condition.

Naomi's Proverbs

It takes all kinds of people to make a world.

Children and Parenting

Naomi's Proverbs

Back in my day children always listened to their parents because when they didn't something bad always happened.

Naomi's Proverbs

I don't uphold my children when they do something wrong.

Naomi's Proverbs

I'm a modern mother. I try to keep up with the times.

A Black Mother Speaks   Page 51

Naomi's Proverbs

Don't ever talk about someone else's child because you never know what your own will do.

Naomi's Proverbs

We always took our children to the circus and things for children so they wouldn't grow up backwards and wouldn't know nothing.

Naomi's Proverbs

All my children seemed to have problems at the same time.

Naomi's Proverbs

My sister Doris and I were just determined to make our marriages work. We had too many kids.

Naomi's Proverbs

I've been your age before and I was fast so you can't fool me about anything.

A Black Mother Speaks Page 56

Naomi's Proverbs

Don't put nobody before your children.

A Black Mother Speaks   Page 57

Naomi's Proverbs

You can't pick me and put me down when you feel like it. Some people treat you any kind of way and then turn around and act like they haven't done anything to you. They'll come smiling in your face and will even have the nerve to ask you to help them in some kind of way just like you're stupid.

Naomi's Proverbs

Do what you want to do with your life. You're only here for a short time so make yourself happy.

Naomi's Proverbs

Respect everybody because you never know who might have to bring you a glass of water when you're thirsty.

A Black Mother Speaks

Naomi's Proverbs

Some folks will tell you what they are or are not going to do and turn around and do the exact opposite. You best make up your own mind on things.

Naomi's Proverbs

Don't follow the crowd.
Think for yourself.

A Black Mother Speaks   Page 63

Naomi's Proverbs

I like doing decent and respectable things.

Naomi's Proverbs

The truth will eventually come out.

Naomi's Proverbs

You can't live your life to please other people; you'll be miserable.

Naomi's Proverbs

When your time is up, your time is up.

Naomi's Proverbs

When you dig a ditch for someone else you just as well dig one for yourself.

A Black Mother Speaks   Page 68

Naomi's Proverbs

How do you expect people to know anything when they ain't never been nowhere other than to church and the grocery store?

Naomi's Proverbs

I'm not ever going to shortchange my own self.

A Black Mother Speaks

Naomi's Proverbs

Sometime you have to push yourself even if you don't feel like it. You can't give in to your feelings.

Naomi's Proverbs

Everything ain't always going to go your way.

Naomi's Proverbs

I'm for right.

A Black Mother Speaks   Page 73

Naomi's Proverbs

If you play with a dog long enough, after a while it will kiss you in the mouth.

Naomi's Proverbs

Always leave home fixed up because you never know who you might see in the streets.

When you do drugs you can't hide it. It shows in your face and everybody knows it. You need help.

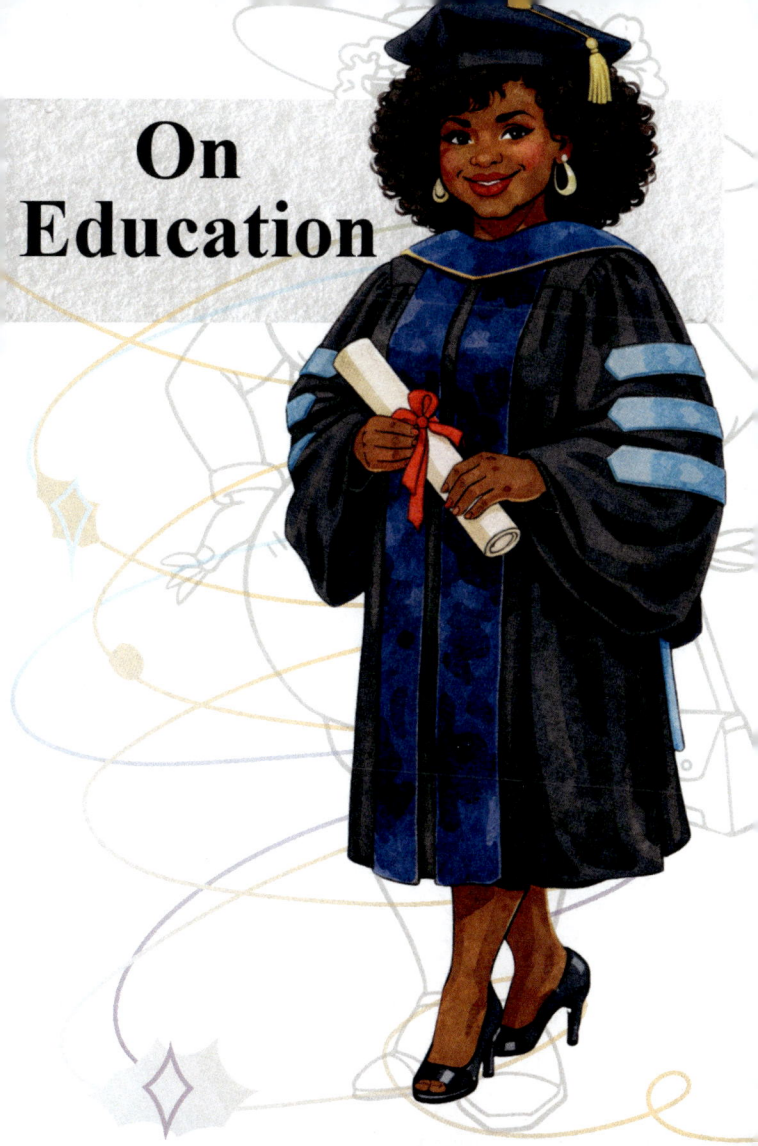

On Education

Naomi's Proverbs

I may not have a college degree, but I have good old-fashioned mother sense. Learn how to do something in life to make a living; if you don't go to college, learn a skill or trade.

Naomi's Proverbs

Most Black people with education act like they're better than other people. I guess if I had to rack my brains as hard as some of them did to get their degree, I would be proud too.

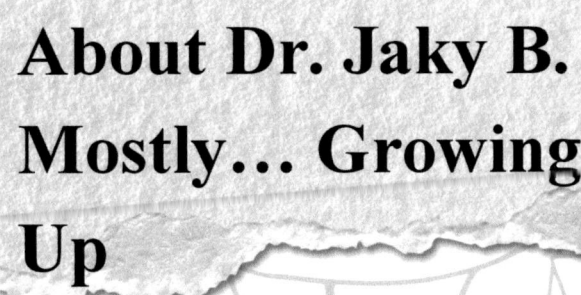

About Dr. Jaky B. Mostly… Growing Up

Jacqueline, Dr. Jaky B., poses with her mother, Naomi, after Easter service in 1963. A former Philadelphia model with impeccable style, Naomi instilled confidence in her daughter by always having her look her best.

Dr. Jaky B., age three, in her family church after winning a queen contest. Guided by her mother's fundraising skill, she was later crowned May Queen at age seven in 1963 at Cedar Lane Elementary, an all-Black school, during the school's May Day celebration.

Top: Jacqueline with her five Maryland brothers and parents. Bottom: Jacqueline and brothers at maternal grandparents home "Down the Neck".

Nicholas S. Banks, Sr.

The entrepreneur dad wiho raised Dr. Jaky B. His vision led to the first entertainment venue in Black Allen. They owned the land and building. Uncles and Cousins built it.

Mom holding me, Dr. Jaky B., in her arms while my oldest brother Nick looks on.

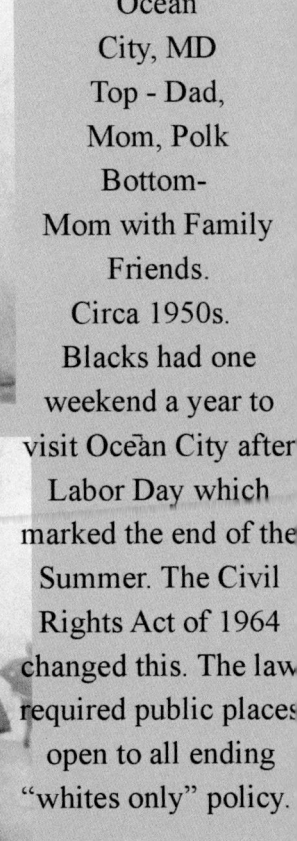

Ocean City, MD
Top - Dad, Mom, Polk
Bottom- Mom with Family Friends.
Circa 1950s.
Blacks had one weekend a year to visit Ocean City after Labor Day which marked the end of the Summer. The Civil Rights Act of 1964 changed this. The law required public places open to all ending "whites only" policy.

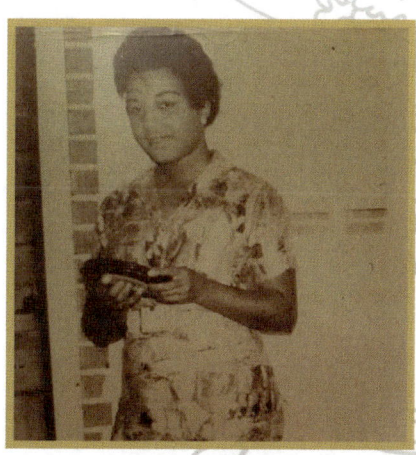

Mom visiting Raymond Polk family relatives in Roanoke, VA. Circa 1960s. Below- my Sweet Sixteen Birthday Party held in my parents' business.

Mom, her six children, one daughter-in-law, two youngest grandchildren. Kendra is the granddaughter with the tongue hanging out. Bottom - our last photo with all six of Mom's children. Me and my five brothers....

Mom/Grandmom in the stripes and six of her 10 siblings on a family trip to Niagara Falls —my son Jody was four. She was the one who organized our family trips, reunions, and gatherings.

Dr. Jaky B. *Mom's oldest sister Mabeline was poisoned at age 16 by a neighbor who had a grudge against her parents. We grew up being told to never eat from anyone's table unless parents approved. All Aunts were approved.*

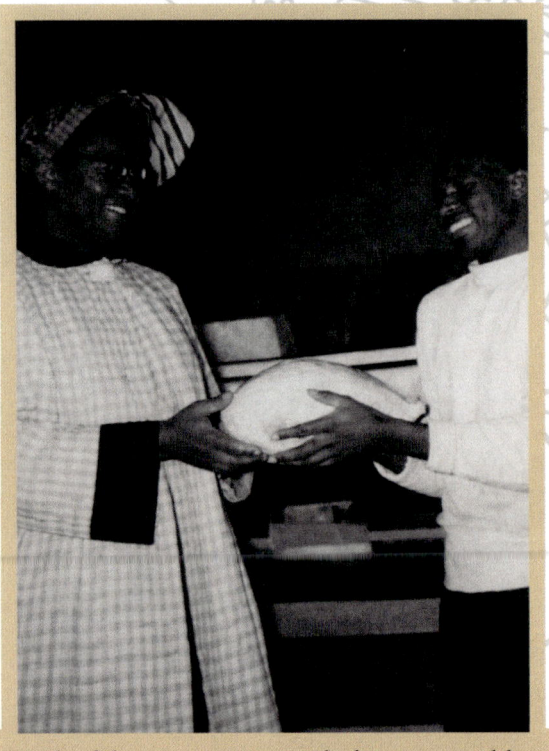

Dad with a customer at their store and beer garden called "Nick's Peaceful Palace. It was mostly a night club with live music, some short order food and groceries. I can still smell the magic marker my mother used to make posters on white paper.

*M*y life work has been about doing things that benefit children and their families. Writing and speaking have played significant roles in how I have connected purpose.
I hail from a rural small village called Allen, located on the Lower Eastern Shore of Maryland. My parents, and neighbors who were more than likely family members, were entrepreneurs, hustlers; Our Allen Black Wall Street.

Growing up folks gathered in the church or in my parents' beer garden.
I detest racism because it denies humanity, hurts children and stifles lives so I actively oppose it. My books, plays, articles, letters, proposals, plans, speeches, use of all media (podcasts, radio and television hosting, and legal battles, etc. all serve as tools to bring awareness, improve lives, spark dialogue, bring change.
I am PWI educated. Towson University. Salisbury University where I was the first Black to earn a MBA, The Johns Hopkins University for a Master of Arts in Teaching with my final career change and Drexel University for a Doctorate of Education .
I want better. So I put the work in with the bit I've been allocated...*I am Dr. Jaky B.*

*K*endra D. Banks, a Baltimore City resident originally from Allen, Maryland, is the President of Royalty Is Black (R.I.B.) and a lifelong artist with over 20 years of community activism. Through storytelling and music, she empowers Black girls helping them see themselves in Black-fantasy worlds while learning content. and life lessons.

Kendra's artistic journey began early—she won a Maryland State PTA award in 4th grade for her original song "I See the Beauty of God." In 2023, she earned two music video awards. Her newest children's single,is "Flow Those ABC's" by The Black Mermaid.

Kendra holds a B.S. from Morgan State University and has trained at elite dance programs including ADF Dance Festival, Bates Dance Festival, and the Martha Graham Dance Program. She is also known for her work as a longtime member of the rock/SKA band The Upstarters.

From appearing on HBO's The Wire and the film Step Up to The Apollo Theatre, Kendra uses her creativity and social entrepreneurship to inspire change.

Made in the USA
Coppell, TX
01 March 2026